D0966788

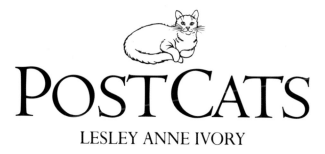

POSTCATS

LESLEY ANNE IVORY

Chronicle Books • San Francisco

The cat likes nice smells such as flowers, spices, perfumes. It also likes nice things to lie on such as silks, satins and furs ... A cat at rest with me in the same room is what I like best. The curl-up in a perfect circle or sometimes with one paw over its eyes as though to shut out the light; the hunker with all four feet tidily tucked under, or the sit-up with its tail neatly tucked around its bottom. The poses I know are sheer vanity, for cats are indeed vain and like to be admired. But they will choose backgrounds and put themselves into positions which they know are admirable. They will hang a paw in what seems to be a wholly casual manner, but you know and they know damn well it is studied. But it is never wrong. Merely by the turn of their heads upon their necks, a half inch or so, they can change the picture and give expression to some inner feeling and, by doing so, set up a glow of appreciation in the watcher.

PAUL GALLICO, *HONOURABLE CAT*

Sages austere and fervent lovers both,
 In their ripe season, cherish cats, the pride
Of hearths, strong, mild, and to themselves allied
In chilly stealth and sedentary sloth.

Friends both to lust and learning, they frequent
Silence, and love the horror darkness breeds.
Erebus would have chosen them for steeds
To hearses, could their pride to it have bent.

Dreaming, the noble postures they assume
Of sphinxes stretching out into the gloom
That seems to swoon into an endless trance.

Their fertile flanks are full of sparks that tingle,
And particles of gold, like grains of shingle,
Vaguely be-star their pupils as they glance.

CHARLES BAUDELAIRE, *Cats*

Bput what are their faults compared with their virtues – with their sense of humour, their fidelity, their dauntless courage (unless they think they've seen a ghost, when they will tear away like so many animated brushes), their playfulness (they will retrieve a piece of paper as many times as you will throw it for them), their conversational powers (if you have Siamese cats you must talk to them a lot), their awareness of themselves so that each one of my eleven knows his own name, their love of people rather than place; their honesty (by which I mean they'll take a lobster from the table in front of you), their continuous passionate interest in all that is going on around them, and their depth of affection, which they are able to show in so many exquisite ways.

COMPTON MACKENZIE, *SIAMESE CATS*

Stately, kindly, lordly friend,
    Condescend
Here to sit by me, and turn
Glorious eyes that smile and burn,
Golden eyes, love's lustrous meed,
On the golden page I read.

All your wondrous wealth of hair
    Dark and fair,
Silken-shaggy, soft and bright
As the clouds and beams of night,
Pays my reverent hand's caress
Back with friendlier gentleness.

Dogs may fawn on all and some
    As they come;
You, a friend of loftier mind,
Answer friends alone in kind!
Just your foot upon my hand
Softly bids it understand.

ALGERNON SWINBURNE, *To a Cat*

Tearaway kitten or staid mother of fifty,
  Persian, Chinchilla, Siamese
Or backstreet brawler – you all have a tiger in your blood
And eyes opaque as the sacred mysteries.

The hunter's instinct sends you pouncing, dallying,
Formal and wild as a temple dance.
You take from men what is due – the fireside saucer,
And give him his – a purr of tolerance.

Like poets you wrap your solitude around you
And catch your meaning unawares:
With consequential trot or frantic tarantella
You follow up your top-secret affairs.

C. DAY-LEWIS, *CAT*

To gain the friendship of a cat is a difficult thing. The cat is a philosophical, methodical, quiet animal, tenacious of his own habits, fond of order and cleanliness, and does not lightly confer his friendship. If you are worthy of his affection, a cat will be your friend but never your slave. He keeps his free will though he loves, and will not do for you what he thinks unreasonable; but if he once gives himself to you, it is with absolute confidence and fidelity of affection. He makes himself the companion of your hours of solitude, melancholy and toil. He will remain for whole evenings on your knee, uttering a contented purr, happy to be with you. Put him down and he will jump up again with a sort of cooing sound that is a gentle reproach; and sometimes he will sit upon the carpet in front of you looking at you with eyes so melting, so caressing, and so human that they almost frighten you, for it is impossible to believe that a soul is not there.

THEOPHILE GAUTIER, *MENAGERIE INTIME*

With slow and confidential pace,
  And parlour-manners on her face,
She creeps to her accustomed place,
  My very perfect little cat;
There, as she curls her body round,
The mat grows consecrated ground;
And sure it shelters, safe and sound,
  A very perfect little cat.

Ah, yes, you look as good as gold
While round that cosy nose you fold
Those paws to keep it from the cold,
  You very perfect little cat!
But let me learn a little more:
What were you doing just before
I heard you mewing at the door,
  My very perfect little cat?

LAURENCE HOUSMAN, *PERFECT LITTLE CAT*

The cat regards the hearthstone as her own,
   Accepts her board and lodging as her due.
She condescends to those whom she has known,
Bestows some small affection on a few.
Allows herself to be caressed by some
And purrs most musically when she is pleased
But never comes unless she wants to come,
She teases, but herself is never teased.
Unchanged throughout the ages she remains
Completely her own master and her form
Stays feline yet she sheaths her claws for gains
While her soft body stays secure and warm,
And on her lips the same enigma smile
She wore when she was worshipped by the Nile.

DOROTHY QUICK, *SONNET TO A CAT*

As the learned and ingenious Montaigne says … 'When my cat and I entertain each other with mutual apish tricks, as playing with a garter, who knows but that I make my cat more sport than she makes me? Shall I conclude her to be simple, that has her time to begin or refuse to play as I myself have? Nay, who knows but that it is a defect of my not understanding her language (for doubtless cats talk and reason with one another), that we agree no better? And who knows but that she pities me for being no wiser than to play with her, and laughs and censures my folly for making sport for her, when we two play together?'

IZAAK WALTON, *THE COMPLEAT ANGLER*

Dear creature by the fire a-purr,
   Strange idol, eminently bland,
Miraculous puss! As o'er your fur
   I trail a negligible hand,

And gaze into your gazing eyes,
   And wonder in a demi-dream
What mystery is it that lies
   Behind those slits that glare and gleam,

An exquisite enchantment falls
   About the portals of my sense;
Meandering through enormous halls
   I breathe luxurious frankincense,

An ampler air, a warmer June
   Enfold me, and my wandering eye
Salutes a more imperial moon
   Throned in a more resplendent sky

Than ever knew this northern shore.
   Oh, strange! For you are with me too,
And I who am a cat once more
   Follow the woman that was you.

With tail erect and pompous march,
   The proudest puss that ever trod,
Through many a grove, 'neath many an arch,
   Impenetrable as a god.

GILES LYTTON STRACHEY, *THE CAT*

A blazing fire, a warm rug, candles lit and curtains drawn, the kettle on for tea . . . and finally, the cat before you, attracting your attention; it is a scene which everybody likes . . . The cat purrs, as if it applauded our consideration, and gently moves its tail. What an odd expression of the power to be irritable and the will to be pleased there is in its face, as it looks up at us! . . . Now she begins to clean herself all over, having a just sense of the demands of her elegant person, beginning judiciously with her paws, and fetching amazing tongues at her hind-hips. Anon, she scratches her neck with a foot of rapid delight, leaning her head towards it, and shutting her eyes, half to accommodate the action of the skin, and half to enjoy the luxury . . . Finally, she gives a sneeze, and another thrust of mouth and whiskers, and then, curling her tail towards her front claws, settles herself on her hind quarters in an attitude of bland meditation . . . Cats at firesides live luxuriously, and are the picture of comfort.

LEIGH HUNT, *THE CAT BY THE FIRE*

Half loving-kindliness and half disdain,
   Thou comest to my call serenely suave,
With humming speech and gracious gestures grave,
In salutation courtly and urbane:
Yet must I humble me thy grace to gain –
For wiles may win thee, but no arts enslave,
And nowhere gladly thou abidest, save
Where nought disturbs the concord of thy reign.
Sphinx of my quiet hearth! who deignst to dwell,
Friend of my toil, companion of mine ease,
Thine is the lore of Ra – and Rameses;
That men forget dost thou remember well,
Beholden still in blinking reveries,
With sombre sea-green gaze inscrutable.

ROSAMUND MARRIOTT WATSON, *TO MY CAT*

Oh cat! I'd say, or pray: be-ooootiful cat! Delicious cat! Exquisite cat! Satiny cat! Cat like a soft owl, cat with paws like moths, jewelled cat, miraculous cat! cat, cat, cat, cat.

She would ignore me at first; then turn her head, silkily arrogant, and half close her eyes for each praise-name, each one separately. And, when I'd finished, yawn, deliberate, foppish, showing an ice-cream pink mouth and curled pink tongue.

Or, deliberate, she would crouch and fascinate me with her eyes. I stared into them, almond-shaped in their fine outline or dark pencil, around which was a second pencilling of cream. Under each, a brush-stroke of dark. Green, green eyes; but in shadow, a dark smoky gold – a dark-eyed cat. But in the light, green, a clear cool emerald. Behind the transparent globes of the eyeball, slices of veined gleaming butterfly wing. Wings like jewels – the essence of wing.

DORIS LESSING, *PARTICULARLY CATS*

In a dim corner of my room for longer than my fancy
   thinks
A beautiful and silent Sphinx has watched me through the
   shifting gloom.

Inviolate and immobile she does not rise she does not stir
For silver moons are naught to her and naught to her the
   suns that reel.

Red follows grey across the air the waves of moonlight
   ebb and flow
But with the Dawn she does not go and in the night-time
   she is there.

Dawn follows Dawn and Nights grow old and all the
   while this curious cat
Lies crouching on the Chinese mat with eyes of satin
   rimmed with gold.

OSCAR WILDE, *THE SPHINX*

He blinks upon the hearth-rug
And yawns in deep content,
Accepting all the comforts
That Providence has sent.

Louder he purrs, and louder
In one glad hymn of praise,
For all the night's adventures,
For quiet, restful days.

Life will go on for ever,
With all that cat can wish;
Warmth, and the glad procession
Of fish, and milk, and fish.

Only – the thought disturbs him –
He's noticed once or twice,
The times are somehow breeding
A nimbler race of mice.

ALEXANDER GRAY, *ON A CAT AGING*

First published in the United States in 1989
by Chronicle Books

Conceived, edited and designed by
Russell Ash and Bernard Higton
Copyright © Russell Ash and Bernard Higton 1989
Illustrations copyright © Lesley Anne Ivory 1989

Printed in Hong Kong by Imago

ISBN 0-87701-639-9

Chronicle Books
275 Fifth Street
San Francisco, California
94103
10 9 8 7 6 5 4

Text extracts from the following sources are reprinted with the kind permission of the publishers and copyright holders stated. Should any copyright holder have been inadvertently omitted they should apply to the publishers who will be pleased to credit them in full in any subsequent editions.

Paul Gallico, *Honourable Cat*, reprinted by permission of Souvenir Press Ltd and Crown Publishers Inc; Laurence Housman,

'Perfect Little Cat', reprinted by permission of the Executors of the Estate of Laurence Housman; Doris Lessing, *Particularly Cats*, reprinted by permission of Michael Joseph Ltd; C. Day Lewis, 'Cat', from *The Poems of C. Day Lewis*, reprinted by permission of the Peters Fraser & Dunlop Group Ltd; Compton Mackenzie, 'Siamese Cats', from *Cat's Company*, reprinted by permission of The Society of Authors as the literary representative of the Estate of Compton Mackenzie.